OPRAH WINFREY

125 Success Lessons You Should Learn From Oprah!

(Inspirational Lessons on Life, Love, Relationships, Self-Image, Career & Business)

--by Tony Rohn

Copyright

Table Of Contents

Chapter 1: Why Should You Learn From Successful People?

Everyone wants to be successful in their life. To be successful in life, one needs to have a positive attitude towards life. Only a positive attitude will help a person achieve great heights in life. The world's most successful people have always risen above their troubles and outperformed their competitors.

Successful people have success mindset. A person who wants to achieve success in his or her life can develop this mindset and can totally change his life.

But **how to develop this success mindset**? To learn this you must study the mindset and habits of successful people.

When you learn the path followed by them to become successful, you can embrace it in your life too. To achieve your life's goals, you must study the achievers' teachings closely, learn the lessons offered and tweak them to use in your own life according to the situations you face.

Learning from successful people is the sure path to success. It is like having a mentor guide you your path. Imagine you are the captain of a ship sailing without a map! **Learning about successful people gives "THE MAP" you need to navigate through the hard waves of life.**

In life, when you are focusing all your energy to become successful, you are bound to incur some obstacles, challenges and failures. By studying successful people you can learn how they overcame their hardships in life and business and thereby you can use those lessons in your own life.

Not all of us have the luxury to have a mentor who is a millionaire or billionaire. Not all of us have the luxury to invest thousands of dollars in self-development / success seminars conducted by great personalities.

But getting their knowledge in a concise form through a book is way easier. It is cheaper than other tools and most valuable. In longterm, you may forget the content taught in a one-to-one coaching session or a seminar – but you can keep a book with you forever, you can keep going through the lessons taught by that person and can study it and apply it in your life without much hassles.

Put your mind to study successful people, put your mind to emulate their success practices, work hard on your goals and keep taking massive actions - I am sure; success will be yours in no time!

Chapter 2: How To Copy Successful People & Become A Success?

The most effective methods of becoming successful in whatever it is you want to achieve, is to copy those who are already successful in your eyes.

Here is a step-by-step strategy to become successful:

1. Surround yourself with successful people
2. Watch, listen to, and learn from successful people so that you can recognize how successful people talk, think, and behave
3. Emulate the habits of successful people so that you too get positive results
4. Read the success stories of others, especially those that you admire who rose to the top from poorer or less successful beginnings
5. Learn even from the failures of others.
6. Continue to learn, and never assume that you know everything.

Chapter 3: Oprah– The Great Inspiration

For many people across the globe, Oprah Winfrey is a great source of inspiration. Oprah touched the lives of millions of people on earth. She taught us abundant life lessons, business lessons and success lessons. Though Oprah's starting stage of life was humble, the kind of success she has achieved is humongous.

Irrespective of caste, creed, race and nationality, her message evokes the inner feelings of millions of human hearts. She is the symbol of courage, confidence, energy and dreams. She was from a very humble background but through hard work and determination, she raced ahead of her competitors and won the toughest race in Media industry irrespective of the negative criticisms she received during her growing years.

Through her unending efforts, through her willpower, through her constant efforts in personal development, through her continuous learning, through her patience, through her raw talent – she won the hearts of millions of Americans and also of the people from various countries spread across the globe.

Oprah redefined beauty. She taught us what real beauty means. She taught us what real beauty is made of. You can shine in your life if you ignite your inner light. You can reach greater heights, if you believe in yourself and work towards your dreams. You can get anything you want, if you put your mind to it. You can be the happiest person, if you know how to be grateful in your life.

She taught us what real beauty looks like – by shining her inner light to this world. She is the greatest women, the greatest human being alive. Her words touch and heal wounded hearts. Her words bring magic to the souls of people with crumbled hearts. Her charisma enlightens the lives of people from all walks of life.

This world is harsh and cruel. If you have to survive in the human race and achieve success, you have to emulate successful people. By studying successful people, by learning what worked for them, by implementing those techniques in your life, by dedicatedly following the footprints of giants – you can win this harsh cruel world.

To achieve massive success, you do not have the advantage of following the beaten path. Time is crucial here. You cannot waste so much time doing your own mistakes and repeating them often to learn a solid life lesson. You need success lessons from the people who have already seen it and done it. By sincerely studying and following the teachings of great leaders and success personas – you can attain success. If you are committed to following your success irrespective of whatever highs and lows you have to go through in life - you can become successful.

To some people success is a destination. To some success is a journey. To become successful – some people set a goal, achieve it and get contented. Likewise there are some who keep setting higher and higher benchmarks for them and don't stop until they achieve it.

To think success as a journey or destination? You cannot argue which is right! But it is essential for you to figure out whether you want success as a destination, as an end goal or you want success as a journey, as a mean goal – as a means to achieve something.

Figure out what success means to you, so that it would be relatively easy for you to study and emulate successful people in your life. To achieve anything you want in life, you need to find your WHY. You have to find your ultimate purpose in doing an activity. Figure out your WHY, follow the blue print of successful people and tirelessly work on it – success will be yours in no time.

Oprah followed a practice vigorously. That is to invest in herself continuously. If you want to win in life, you should make a conscious choice to keep investing in yourself.

It is very easy to get side-tracked by secondary activity. It is very easy to spend your free hours before a TV than reading a self-development book that uplifts your spirit or reading a biography of a world leader that could spark a great idea in you. It is very easy to waste time comparing items to purchase in online shopping websites than using those fruitful hours to take an online course that improves your skill-set. Easy is not the route for success. If you want success you got to work for it – like your life depended on it!

To win in life, to achieve success, to get massive results – you need to take massive actions. If you want to win like your idol, you should deeply study and emulate him or her – in all possible ways.

If you study great personalities, especially the highly successful ones, you can see a common pointer in all of them – that is their passion for work, their eagerness to spend all their energy to get ahead, their ability to forsake everything to pursue that one single thing, their interest to risk everything they have ever earned to go higher and higher. If you want success like the way you will want to breathe when your head is stuck deep in water, you will do anything to achieve it. Success is your duty and to be successful is the basic yearning of every human being.

Oprah is an amazing individual. She is one of the most beloved women in this world. She is the first African billionaire and an exceptional philanthropist. Her success was beyond limits and bounds. She achieved her massive success through her will power and determination and great amounts of work – day in and day out.

People follow Oprah in all walks of their lives. Be it a young kid or a working women or a college student, or a mom or a grandmother – she has attracted everyone though her amazing personality. She vibrates on screen and off screen. Her aura and energy is so miraculous.

If you have chosen to read this book, it means you want to be successful in life and also you want to learn the success secrets offered by Oprah for your life. I applaud you for taking your life seriously. I applaud you for putting in the effort to become successful. I applaud you for taking the necessary starting steps to become successful.

Now, let us learn more about Oprah Winfrey's inspirational success lessons on life, career and business. You will also learn about how you can use those success lessons inorder to have a successful life. Are you ready to get motivated? Are you ready to become a successful person? Are you ready to take your life to another level?

Here we go! Let's get started...

Inspirational Lessons on Life, Love, Relationships, Self-Image, Career & Business from Oprah Winfrey

Chapter 4: Oprah On How To Start Everyday with Positivity

Every day brings a chance for you to draw in a breath, kick off your shoes and dance

Life is magical if you know your worries are not going to last forever. Each day and each moment is a blessing. It is an opportunity for you to cherish the moments offered to you. Every day brings in itself a promise for betterment. Every day whispers – 'Life is not going to be the same'. You can live the best life possible – if you put your mind to it. You can live the life of your dreams – if you consciously make choices towards living your dreams.

Every day brings in itself exceptional gifts for you. You can make or break the day – the choice is yours. You can make a decision based on love or fear. The amount of effort and thought process is the same.

So why not bet on love than fear? Why not take a chance to be more of yourself today? Why not live your best self not tomorrow, not day after but today? Why not do the things today that make your heart rejoice? Why not believe in yourself, believe in your capabilities, and believe in your dreams today? Why not take mindful decisions to live a better life today? The choice is yours. Every day brings to you a promise – a promise to live more, live beyond. Are you making the right choice today?

Chapter 5: Oprah On The Law Of Attraction

You get in life what you have the courage to ask for

You are the captain of your ship. If you do not take control – who will? In life you get to choose what you want to become. You get to choose whom to live with. You get to choose what to study. You get to choose your dreams. Nobody else have the control over you. Your choices are yours. You are the decision maker. You are the authority figure for your life. If you do not take control over yourself, if you do not take control over your life, then you will be controlled by other people, circumstances, events and incidents.

If you want to have a successful life, you have to own it – you should become responsible for your life – if you rely on blame-game on others, you are never going to win. Likewise, if you want to have a successful career, you have to own it. Want a salary hike? Know your boss's door and ask him face-to-face. Want a better, more loving relationship? Talk to your spouse, one-to-one. Want to have other people respect you? Show them how they have to handle you. You will get in life what you ask of it.

Some people do not have the courage to ask their lives of what they want – so they will end up being mediocre individuals. They settle with ordinary jobs, ordinary paychecks, ordinary relationships and ordinary life. Remember, you can do more than that. You can choose to rise above the mediocrity by simply taking control of your life and asking more from you to become more.

When you think success as your duty and responsibility – you will start asking more from life, you will start having the courage to face things one-to-one and enrich yourself through every experience. What is stopping you taking control of your life? What is stopping you asking more from life? What is stopping you become more? What is stopping you living your best life possible?

The answer is simple. It is YOU! You make the choices that could elevate your life to another level or that could take you to live a gutter-life. Develop the courage to demand more from you, to demand more from your life – that's the success secret to win in anything you want - be it your life, career, business or relationships.

Chapter 6: Oprah On Getting Things Done

Cheers to a new year and another chance for us to get it right

All of us take New Year resolutions only to fail at it miserably within first few days from the start of that New Year. Do you remember the time you want to trim down those excess fats in your chest and belly areas and eagerly were waiting for the start of New Year to enroll in a gym? What happened in a month? Where did your motivation go? Why did you forsake the decision to exercise, trim down those extra pounds, have a beautiful healthy body, get that dream job, get that dream girl of yours?

If you believe new year is another chance for you to make your mistakes right again, if you believe you can set right your broken life in the upcoming year – take a conscious choice to plan it and work on it. Do not break your goals for the year. Every year is a chance for you to grow internally and externally. Every year is an opportunity for you to grow spiritually, physically, mentally and emotionally.

Be mindful about not getting side tracked by secondary activities. Develop a goal setting mindset and take massive amounts of actions to achieve your goals. If you vigorously go after creating success in your life, career, business or personal relationships – you can win it if you give your heart and soul for it. If you work on it consistently – you can achieve anything you want in life.

If you want to make something right this year, make it happen. Do not give excuses to yourself. Analyze your life; take an inventory of what is working and what is not. If you feel something is going right, take that path and keep going with full momentum. If you feel something is not right, just take a U-turn. Allow your intuition to guide you. Allow your inner power to take you places. Allow your inner genius to work on yourself and on your goals.

Remember, every year is another chance for you to get your life right again. Be it a messy relationship, be it a nasty argument with your boss, be it an emotional tangle with your parents – you can make things right again, by putting your mind to work on it.

Chapter 7: Oprah On The Importance Of Surrounding Yourself With Positive People

Surround yourself only with people who are going to take you higher

Most of us do not aim higher because we are surrounded by people who do not have high hopes or dreams or goals for their lives. It might be your parents, your spouse or your friends – you are the product of the 5 people you spend most time with.

If you are surrounding yourself with people who dream high, who push through difficulties to achieve greatness in life, I am sure, just by association, you will become someone who set high bars in life. If you are surrounding yourself with mediocre people with mediocre mindset, I assure you, you would end up being mediocre forever in your life.

To go places, you need to have people who will raise you up. You need people who will be a support for your dreams. You need people who will push you higher and higher through their constructive criticism. You need people who will motivate you to be an 'awesome you'.

You might have great dreams and goals but if you do not have the right people around, chances are meager that you are going to achieve your goals. You need a partner, family, friends' circle – who will understand you for who you are, who will understand your great dreams, who will be ready to openly hurt you and silently care you inorder to see you achieve your goals in life.

Take a moment and inventory the people that surround you. Do they raise you high or they bring you down? Do they give you constructive criticism or break you down by constant negative criticisms? Do they have great dreams for themselves? Do they push their comfort zones inorder to achieve their dreams? What is the kind of people surrounding you now? Analyze and understand.

Also make a conscious choice to surround yourself with people who will raise you higher in life. You have to decide today to be around people who will want to see you at the top. For a dreamer like you, for someone who has great expectations in life – you need people who will inspire you to achieve your goals and living a great life.

Chapter 8: Oprah On The Importance Of Celebrating Life

The more you praise and celebrate your life, the more there is in life to celebrate

How true! Do you appreciate the things in your life? Do you appreciate your healthy body that functions all its duty accurately from the moment you are conceived till now? Do you appreciate your sound mind that helps you navigate life effectively? Do you appreciate your spirit that keeps pushing you to realize more of you?

When was the last time you felt happy for the little touch of your kid? When was the last time you felt cheerful for getting an appreciation from your boss? When was the last time you felt awesome by the romantic cuddle of your spouse? If you are appreciative of the things you have in your life, if you are appreciative of the cherishing moments you encounter unexpectedly, if you are appreciative of the quality time you spend with your family – life will start giving you more of it.

Only if you start celebrating your life, your life will start to celebrate you. You should first give to receive in return. You must make the effort to be mindful to be happy for the simple things in your life. Take a moment, feel the bliss and do the happy dance in your mind. It will change the way you feel. This simple exercise will elevate your mood exponentially and makes you feel happier. See your life as something more meaningful, as something graceful, as something to celebrate.

If you keep thinking about negative things, if you keep thinking about everything that went wrong in your life, if you keep thinking about all the things that never worked out – you are going to end up as a negative mindset loser. If you start celebrating your life, there will be more for you to celebrate in life. If you start blaming your life, there will be more for you to blame in life.

Be it your relationships, love life or professional life – think about everything that life has offered you. Think about all the great gifts you have in your life, business, career and relationships and start appreciating each and everything mindfully and soulfully.

Start counting your blessings and be appreciative of your life. You will find more and more things to appreciate in all the walks of your life!

Chapter 9: Oprah On Letting Go

Breathe. Let go. And remind yourself that this very moment is the only one you know you have for sure

Sometimes we feel overwhelmed. It might be due to pressure or stress we developed in our job or at home. That overwhelming sensation might have been caused by a person we love and care. At the times of stress, we feel like everything is toppling down, everything is crumbling to pieces; everything is going far away from us.

It might be the love of your life who hurt you for no reason. It might be your coworker who works against your back at office. It might be your kid who does nasty things unknowingly. It might be because of any strong or silly reasons – but at those times we feel fear, we feel as though everything, our life, our jobs, our relationship, this world – is going to end.

But is that so? Take a moment to turn back in your life when you thought about an incidence and you felt "This is it. My life is done". Fast forward, you are now feeling

"Nope. That is not the end. My life wasn't done because of that incidence. It is funny how I thought about that incidence then"!

Life is like that. The overwhelming moments we feel, would not be so overwhelming when we think about that same incidence, after a week or after a month. But still we do not think rationally at the times of stress! We, human beings are not wired properly to think clearly under stress or pressure or anxiety – atleast the majority of us aren't!

At overwhelming moments – try to breathe deeply and let go of the internal pressures you feel. Keep telling yourself, "will I feel the same amount of vigorous emotion if I look back this incidence a week / month / year from now". Keep repeating this question in yourself and take slow deep breathes. You will feel alive and alright again sooner than you can imagine. This exercise is such a powerful one to come out of the moments that tries to engulf us.

We are fearful of the future. We suffer because we keep worrying about what future holds. Will I have this job? Will I get that promotion? Will I be able to buy a house? Will I be able to care for a child? Will I be able to get an understanding husband? Will I be able to get a loving life partner? We keep repeating these questions in us without understanding, this is the only moment you own, you do not have power over your past or future happenings.

If you keep worrying about the things on which you do not have control over, you develop the worry habit that soon turns into anxiety and depression. Whenever you find yourself getting into the worry-habit, stop yourself right there, take deep breathes and remind yourself that this is the only moment you have control over. This is the moment to think about. Worrying about future, keep thinking about how future is going to turn up is a total waste of your time.

Chapter 10: Oprah On Handling Challenging Times

I trust that everything happens for a reason, even if we are not wise enough to see it

This is one of my favorite quotes from Oprah! In our lives we feel such strong emotions at times due to various ill comings. It might be a loss of a loved one. It might be a sudden break up of your 4 years loving relationship. It might be the cheating of your spouse. It might be anything that makes you crumble from inside out. During these moments, we feel powerless beyond measures and most of the times do not know what to do, think, see or look forward to.

During these moments of fear, doubt and worry – it is better to think that everything happens for a reason. Today's tragedy of our life can be our tomorrow's greatest life lessons. Remembering every incidence occur for a higher purpose helps you in giving yourself to the hands of the great power and being reassured of 'everything is going to be okay again'.

You might not be wise enough today to see what that incidence got to teach you in the near future. The greatest blows of our lives make you stronger than you ever were in the past. If you learn to face the hard things of today with energy and with the thinking that this event in my life is painful for me to go through but to seek my higher self I need this lesson – you will become fine-tuned individual who faces his wars bravely and carries his scars like a medal.

Chapter 11: Oprah On Integrity

Real integrity is doing the right thing, knowing that nobody is going to know whether you did it or not

Do the things you got to do – irrespective of somebody is policing you or not. Most people fail in personal and professional lives is because they are not willing to do the things they must do – unless they are monitored by someone else. Most of us feel we need not do something unless there is a social currency involved in it.

There is a saying "your real character is what you are when nobody is watching you"!

So live a life of total integrity. Be true to yourself. Do not do something for the sake of it. Do not do something because that is what expected of you by society. Do not do something because your neighbor John did it. Your real character shows when you are doing the things that you need not to do but still you put in the effort to do them – because that is the right thing to do.

In most relationships, one partner will be the giver and another will be the receiver. They do not understand that for a relationship to win each has got to contribute 101% of their time, energy, communication, love and bonding. Each one must be willing to do whatever is required inorder to make the relationship not only work but make it successful. You have to give 101% of yourself if you want the best romantic, loving relationship in the world. You may not required to do the simple things that is needed but if you do with all integrity, you will win!

The same goes for your job. Do you do that work just because your manager is bossing around, pushing you all the time to do and complete that task? Do you do that work and show it off just because your eyes are on the prize of a salary hike? Do not do something only because there is someone to question you if it is not been done. Do the things you got to do, because there is the inner YOU in yourself who will question.

Chapter 12: Oprah On Finding Your True Calling

I've come to believe that each of us has a personal calling that's as unique as a fingerprint – and that the best way to succeed is to discover what you love and then find a way to offer it to others in the form of service, working hard and also allowing the energy of the universe to lead you.

You have a purpose in life. You are here on this earth to do something that only you can do. It might be a grandeur purpose that improves the world or it might be a targeted purpose that affects your community positively or it might be a humble purpose that fulfills and enriches your family.

It is your responsibility to find your life's purpose. It is your responsibility to keep working on it. It is your responsibility to share your gifts with this world.

There is a greatest artist in you. There is a greatest musician in you. There is a greatest architect in you. There is a greatest teacher in you. There is a greatest social activist in you. There is a greatest carpenter in you. There is a greatest mom or dad in you. You are blessed with a personal calling that only you can fulfill and it is your responsibility to find out what it is.

Take some peaceful moments for yourself. Get away from mobile phones, internet and social media and all the outer chatters. Sit in a quiet place with a pen and a paper. Write down everything your heart desires to do. Keep writing for atleast 20 continuous minutes without a break. Suddenly you will start writing about the things you truly longed to do and to your surprise it may sound and feel like you've always wanted to do that, only that one thing all your life.

Figure out that thing and start doing it. Your gifts are needed for this world. This world is waiting to discover what you got to offer. You have the power to make this world a better place – in your own way. If you find out your purpose and constantly be in touch with it, if you work on it and share your innate talents and naturally blessed gifts with this world – you will be living the life on a higher plane. You will be living a life of fulfillment and success!

Chapter 13: Oprah On Handling Relationships

If a man wants you, nothing can keep him away. If he doesn't want you, nothing can make him stay

Are you the clinging type or you analyze the situation and let go of the man or woman you are so in love with? I am not here to judge you or pass judgments; I am here to help you realize yourself more clearly.

The biggest lesson in love, relationship is to let go of the person if he or she doesn't want to stay in it. Take few minutes together and discuss your hearts out. Communicate what is working and what is not – if it is workable, if you both can make it work, if you both can make it an awesome relationship again – well, go ahead and do it. But if you both think this is not going to work, what is the fun in clinging for the sake of it. There is always another Mr.Right or Ms.Right coming your way.

Be with a partner who values you for who you are – not for your beauty, not for your money, not for your social status. He should respect and love you for your true self than the outer things. Go for a man or woman who sees deeper in you. It is true that attraction happens with outer looks, but to enjoy a relationship long-term you need a person who will be contented not only with your looks but your inner soul as well.

So do not waste your energy in clinging, do not spoil your self-respect, self-image and self-esteem by going after someone who is not worth your time and efforts. You might love that person with all your heart, if you know for sure that he or she is not going to return your love, it is a futile effort.

The best thing to do is to move on and keep looking for the right one to come, keep your search to your ideal man than just selecting someone randomly. Give a shot to people who shine with their inner lights, don't judge someone just with their looks – you will find the right partner in no time.

Chapter 14: Oprah On Making Your Dreams A Reality

The biggest adventure you can ever take is to live the life of your dreams

Life is a roller coaster ride. You keep bumping into highs and lows. But if you are living the life of your dreams – it is worth it! Many people go through life as though it is a mundane activity. They do not have the fire for life. They do not do things mindfully or look into the future and envision a better life for them. They keep blaming the government, their family, their spouse for why things are not working out for them.

Dreaming up a good life and taking all the necessary action steps to live the life of your dreams is what you got to do. If you want to be successful in life – be it your personal life, your relationships, your job, your business – whatever the area of focus may be – if you dream it, you can do it.

Dream up a loving relationship. Dream up working the job you love. Dream up being successful in your business venture. Dream up getting that college degree you've always wanted. Dream up reaching that salary benchmark you've been longing all your life. Remember – if you dream it, you can do it.

Living the life of your dreams is a blessing. Yes, it is a thrilling adventure. When you are living the life of your dreams, you will know for sure – you are the chosen one, you are a winner.

Don't get side tracked by fears and doubts. Believe in yourself and dream a better life for you. It is your responsibility to have the best of everything. It is your duty to be successful. So commit to dreaming a better life for you and take massive actions to achieve your dreams. There is nothing more serene and pleasurable than living the life you envisioned in your mind.

Everyone wants to ride with you in the limo, but what you want is someone who will take the bus with you when the limo breaks down.

Take life boldly. Have the courage to dream big. Do not give importance to the little voice that belittles you saying "who are you kidding? Can you really do that?". Stop that voice becoming a better version of YOU. Keep dreaming great dreams and keep working on your dreams through continuous humungous action. You are destined to become successful.

Chapter 15: Oprah On The Importance Of Gratitude

Be thankful for what you have, you will end up having more. If you concentrate on what you don't have, you will never, ever have enough.

Are you thankful for the roof over your head? Are you thankful for the 3 healthy uninterrupted meals you are getting every day? Are you thankful for the clean drinking water at the turn of your tap? Are you thankful for living in a country that is richest in the world? Are you thankful for the loving partner you have? Are you thankful for the beautiful family you are gifted with? Are you thankful for the energetic healthy body of yours?

Be thankful for everything in your life. For what you consider as a simple thing is a luxury somewhere else. To be grateful for your simple and marvelous gifts is a wonderful meditation practice. Feeling stressed? Want to relax yourself? Want to feel more joy in your heart?

Do just this: Take out a pen and a paper or if you are a techie, open your word processor and start writing everything you are grateful for that moment. It might be a simple thing like a coffee at starbucks or a big thing like buying a house – whatever it may be, it doesn't matter how big the thing you are grateful for – what matters is that 'you are **grateful** for that thing at that moment with all your heart and soul'. This simple exercise will change your mood totally, relaxes you and makes you appreciate your life more each day.

Chapter 16: Oprah On Handling Failures

Turn your wounds into wisdom

We all have wounds. Do we carry them as medals like a war hero? Or succumbing to their powers and keep thinking about them over and over and spoiling our current life?

Your wounds will pain you. Even after the pain dissipates, the wound heals, the scars remain. The haunted past of your life will remain in your heart and soul forever. But the question is, Are you going to give power over you? Are you going to keep feeding your fears and doubts and worries about your past mistakes and past wounds?

You have a choice to make. You have the power to turn your wounds into wisdom. You have the responsibility to take life more positively. If life throws bricks at you, catch them and build a wall for yourself. We all face with so many tragic incidents in our lives. Some events empower us, some events engulf us.

The lesson you have to take to your heart is "your fears and doubts will haunt you, only if you give power to them". When you keep visiting and revisiting your past that obstacles your future growth – you are paving a path to failure. You have to take control over your life. It is your responsibility to turn your wounds into lessons for the future.

Your past might be ugly. Your past might be painful. Your past might have the power to ruin your life forever. But keep reminding yourself that you are not going to give that power to your past. You are the decision maker here. You are the authority figure who chooses what to feed. You can feed your fears or you can feed your vision.

Learn to forget the past. Learn not to revisit it unless you have to draw lessons and conclusions. Just keep your past / your wounds as a reference point to steer ahead to a great future. Do not keep your wounds as your blueprint. Turn your wounds into wisdom, that is how a winner is made – that is how winning is done!

Chapter 17: Oprah On Choosing The Right People

If friends disappoint you over and over, that's in large part your own fault. Once someone has shown a tendency to be self-centered, you need to recognize that and take care of yourself. People aren't going to change simply because you want them to.

We can't choose our family but we can choose our friends.

We can decide with whom we are going to stay as friends. We can decide who can be our friends. If you have a negative circle of friends, they are not going to help you in your pursuit of greatness. Your mediocre friends with little minds will keep pulling you down and never take a moment to understand your dreams. Your current friends with no dreams will never help you realize your own grandeur goals.

It is your responsibility to inventory the kind of people you are spending your time with. To whom are you sharing your inner core? To whom are you sharing your highs and lows of life? To whom are you sharing your utmost secrets? You are caring and sharing but are they doing the same thing? If you are around self-centered people who always keep their desires and demands as a priority, it is better to stay away or create a new friends circle who are in-line with your thoughts, goals, aims and dreams.

To live a purposeful life, to achieve massive success – you need to surround yourself with such people who will wish for you more and most in life, who will raise you up and who will shoulder you in all your glory and pains. You need people who have great dreams for themselves. When you are around such people, you can feel the positive aura and energy of life.

Do you have that kind of friends? If you do, cheers! Keep nourishing their relationship. If you don't, it's high-time you form new friendships with like-minded individuals with growth oriented mindset.

Life wants you to win. Life wants you to succeed at your calling. It is your duty to pay attention and act accordingly. To be successful in life, you need friends who will uplift you to reach your higher self. Choose to have those friends in your life!

Chapter 18: Oprah On Decision Making

One of the hardest things in life to learn are which bridges to cross and which bridges to burn.

There was a Chinese captain who wanted to win a war against a dynasty so much that he burnt all their ships that contained the necessities to survive – including food, hut everything. He told his soldiers "You have no choice now. You either win this war, get to live or lose this war and die"! The soldiers fought with all their might that the legend says they won the war 17 continuous times.

We are not good with making decisions. If I ask you to choose one among two products that is exactly similar in all the features – you will take a lot of time to figure out which one to choose. Our decision making nerves, keeps analyzing, analyzing and over analyzing and gets into what psychologists' calls as "analysis paralysis"!

So we end up choosing either the bad one or we choose nothing at all. In our day to day lives we face this confrontation all the time. To choose this dress or that!

To choose this ice cream or that! We are constantly bombarded with trivial decision makings every single day.

It is okay if we fail in our decisions with the things that do not affect our lives. But imagine the kind of effect your decisions will have on the things that affect your life? To choose this man or that? To choose to have this baby or abort? To choose this job or that? –It is very tough to decide when the choosing involves "life changing moments"!

Basically, we humans are risk averse in nature. We fail to lose. But to get ahead in life, we have to choose one thing over another. In choosing the right thing lies our success and in choosing the wrong one lies our failure. Choosing is an art. Only some people are born with it, others have to learn it on the go of life. If you want to learn the art of choosing and make better decisions with your life:

I suggest you to read:

- Predictably Irrational by Dan Ariely
- The Art of Choosing by Sheena Iyengar

Chapter 19: Oprah On The Power Of Belief

You don't become what you want, you become what you believe

This is absolute truth! You are what you feed your mind. You are what you keep thinking. You are what you think you are. In Bhagavad Gita, Lord Krishna says "You Are Your Thoughts"!

If you think you are a success, you will become a success. If you think you are a failure, you will become a failure. Your mind is like water. It takes the shape of whichever vessel you pour in. If you keep feeding your mind with garbage – what you will have there? The result will be garbage! If you feed your mind with positive, nourishing, enriching, success thoughts – the result will be success!

If you want to become that someone, you have to believe that you can become that someone and until you believe you can become that someone you would not succeed at the task in hand.

Believe in yourself. Believe in your dreams and goals. Believe in your higher purpose. Believe in your calling. You might want to become a hundred things but what you believe is what you will become. If you believe yourself as a winner, you will become a winner. If you believe yourself as a loser, you will become a loser. Train your mind for success and success will be yours!

Chapter 20: Oprah On Confidence

You get to know who you really are in a crisis

Tough times shows us what me are made up of inside. During tough times you can understand whether you are facing the moment or looking for ways to flee from it.

Many people act as though they are the bravest people in the world but during the moment of crisis they turn their back and run away from the problem instead of facing it head on. Some people look very humble and naïve but they will have the ability and strength to handle the problem / crisis or undesired situations effectively than anyone else.

If you are someone who wants to walk a rosy life, you will never learn to face critical situations or crisis moments. If you want to learn and grow in life, you have to face and overcome hard times. For you to know whether your inside is made up of rock or sponge, you should be ready to face crisis and should learn the strategies and tactics to face it one-to-one and overcome it triumphantly.

For you to win in personal and professional life, you must face a lot of crisis situations and you must learn the art of crisis management. Your ability to win in life totally depends on how effective you are in handling critical situations ad hard times that life throws at you when you least expect it.

Chapter 21: Oprah On Reading Uplifting Books

Some women have a weakness for shoes... I can go barefoot if necessary. I have a weakness for books.

I am a book-nerd and this is one of my favorite quotes.

Reading is an awesome practice. Once you get into the habit of reading, once you dedicatedly follow through, once you understand and experience the joys of reading, once you start living the thousand lives possible for you, once you know you can vicariously travel the world, once you know this world is your experimental lab, once you start experiencing amazing things in your life – then you will treat reading books as not just another practice but like something more valuable than your life.

Reading is not just a hobby to some people. Reading is above and beyond. Reading helps some readers go beyond the miseries of their lives. Reading helps some people live extraordinary lives that are not possible in their mundane reality.

Reading allows a cripple to walk; he can experience it in his mind, when reading a book that has similar hero like him. Reading allows a coward to fight the evil doers. Reading makes a kid feel like a superhero.

Reading changes you. Reading gives you wings. It gave me wives – Yes! Reading gave me wings. I attribute all my today's learning and success and accomplishments to the books I read. If I haven't become a reader early on, I can tell you, I would not have become who I am today.

You must read. Develop the habit of reading because reading touches you. Reading touches your soul so deeply. I don't think even love can touch you so deeply. Reading takes you to a whole new plane. Reading allows you experience a thousand different thoughts and a thousand different lives.

Can you live a hundred lives in this lifetime?

Can you experience all the experiences of people spread across the world – within one lifetime?

Can you learn what it feels like to be an Indian, an American or an African – within one lifetime?

Can you understand the livelihoods of all the people in the world – within one lifetime?

Can you feel their feelings, their happiness and worries and fears and sorrows – within this one lifetime?

Reading allows you to experience this and more.

Through reading you become someone who is your higher self. You become a better person.

You become someone your parents, your spouse, your siblings, your friends and your community look upto. Reading is a boon for you because it gives you the ability to feel a million feelings.

Imagine the emotions you go through while reading a fiction. The guilt, the love, the passion, the betrayal, the friendship you feel when you read a book. Can any other practice offer you all these experiences at the comfort of sitting on your sofa sipping a cup of coffee?

Through reading you can live the life of a King or Queen. Through reading you can become a Butterfly. Through reading you can live and feel a magical life.

Through reading you can speak to genies. Through reading you can go on an adventure trip.

Through reading you can become a master sorcerer, trying magic tricks on people and on the world. Through reading good books, you can experience love and romance and relationships that you do not have the chance to experience in your real life.

Reading offers you a chance to experience the lives of thousands of people you will never meet, you will never hear about. **Reading offers you your greatness**. You are not just one among the rat racers. You are someone unique. Since you read, since you have consciously chosen to become a reader, you rise above the plateau!

Chapter 22: Oprah On Overcoming Setbacks

Challenges are gifts that force us to search for a new center of gravity. Don't fight them. Just find a new way to stand

Challenges are gifts in disguise. You get to know who you are while handling a challenging situation. You can touch-base with your inner core when you are handling a problem situation.

If you learn to face the challenges life throws at you effectively, you can win in life. Handling challenges needs positive mindset and an audacious attitude. Only a hustler loves challenges; a loser looks for conformity.

To be successful in business, life, career or your relationship – you need the hustle muscle. You need the strong mindset and willpower to overcome every challenge life offers you. You should be strong enough to break through every obstacle life puts in your way.

If you see a problem as a problem – you will never find ways to solve it. You should cultivate the habit of seeing problems and challenges as an opportunity to learn and grow in your life. Be it your professional front or personal front, if you learn the art of problem solving, success will be at your feet! Consider challenges as opportunities. Consider problems as growth instruments.

People who love challenges are the ones who win this world. People who take risks are the ones who live a life beyond limits. People who face challenges head-on are the ones who are successful in life.

Whatever the situation you may face, if you develop a strong mindset and a strong will – you can overcome any tough challenge or situation. Don't fight your challenges, do not run away from them – face them head on and that's how you win!

Chapter 23: Oprah On Living Your Passion

Your true passion should feel like breathing; it's that natural

If you do the things you love in your life, you would know this. If you are working in a job you love, you won't feel burned out or under pressure – your work will feel smooth, your work doesn't feel like work anymore, it becomes your second nature, it comes to you so naturally that you would love to do it even for no money.

The same is true if you are living a life of your dreams. If you are living the life that is based on the personal choices you made, you would feel such a responsibility for your life that you would love each and every day. You might be a happy mom raising beautiful kids, you might be a business executive working on your entrepreneurial career, you might be an artist making an exceptional creative work – if you love what you do, you will feel the vibration of happiness and fulfillment in everything you do through your work.

So do the things you love so you don't feel like working anymore. If work feels like work, you are doing it wrong. You have to find your purpose and do everything you must do inorder to work on your passion constantly – this fills your heart with much joy that you will live a better life realizing your greatest dreams.

If you have doubts whether you've found your true passion or not – ask yourself "**am I really happy doing what I am doing now**"? – This question can help you analyze yourself and thereby assist you make the right decision for your life. When you work on your passion, you will become a creator, you wouldn't be a consumer anymore. You will become one with the flow!

Chapter 24: Oprah On Self-Worth

When you undervalue what you do, the world will undervalue who you are

If you want this world to respect you, you have to teach it HOW! If you undervalue yourself – if you undervalue what you do – what you get in return is what you put in. When you claim yourself as a failure, this world will ensure you become one and stay a failure. If you say you are working in a mean job, getting mean paycheck – this world will ensure you stay mean.

It is your responsibility to know your Self-worth. It is your responsibility to portray yourself respectfully – to this society, to your family, to your spouse, to your kids, to your parents, to your co-workers and to your boss.

The world will only give you in return what you gave in the first place. Are you giving negative statements like you are doing a menial job and going to end up nowhere – this world will ensure what you wish for comes to fruition. So be aware of what you think and say about yourself and about your work. When you undervalue yourself, when you undervalue the things you do for a living – you are ultimately undervaluing everything life has got to offer you!

Be proud of your work. Be proud of who you are. Keep your chin high. Keep your self-respect intact. Your self-image is what the world mirrors to you. If what you see in yourself is a cat - that is what you will see in the reflection of this world. If what you see in yourself is a tiger - that is what you will see in the reflection of this world.

If you degrade or undervalue your work, you are teaching the world how to treat you, you are teaching the world that your work means nothing to you and that is what you are going to get in return. Value what you do. Value who you are. This is an important success mantra.

Chapter 25: Oprah On Embracing Fears & Failures

Go ahead. Fall down. The world looks different from the ground.

From our early childhood we are taught not to fail. In schooling, in college, in work, in business, in life – we are told to become a successful person. If you fail in your exams, your parents see yourself as a failure, if you fail in getting your college degree, your parents see yourself as somebody who is destined to fail in life, if you fail in your business, people see you as somebody who is not worthy enough to run a business. But they do not know the pain you went through.

The people who think You as a failure, do not know that you are walking a different path. The people who think You as a failure, do not know that you might have failed this time, but you will draw enough lessons from your failures and push forward with all might to go greater heights.

Not every successful person is humble – somehow along the way of their success journey head-weight sneaks into them. The fear of failure is essential if you want to be successful. The fear of failure is needed for you so that you will be able to march ahead faster and better.

Sometimes in life, you will fail, but that's okay. Nobody is a constant failure. Use your failures as stepping stones. Use your failures as life's important success lessons. Even when you encounter a thousand failures in the path of your dreams, dust yourself and show up the next time – that is how winning is done! Remember you are born to be successful and the failures you encounter in your personal and professional lives are only temporary.

What is failure for other people should be a new perspective, a new lesson, another stepping stone to your destination. If you want to develop your hustle muscle through failure, here is an exercise for you: "Do the one thing you think you cannot do. Fail at it. Try again. Do better."

Chapter 26: Oprah On Following Your Instinct

Your gut is your inner compass. Whenever you have to consult with other people for an answer, you're headed in the wrong direction.

A few years ago, I was faced with a big life crossroads. I wanted to choose my path in the most rational way possible, so I made a weighted chart with all of the positives and negatives, analyzed the data, and determined the "right" choice.

But something didn't feel right.

Oprah would have told me to go with my gut. She's a strong believer in her instincts, saying they're "where true wisdom manifests itself." She's made her big decisions (like deciding to retire from 'The Oprah Winfrey Show') just based on a gut feeling.

When you need to make the important decisions in your life, collect all the data possible, process that information logically but make sure that your end result is always acknowledging what your gut instinct tells you. Our gut instinct has saved us all these millions of years from the greater forces that are beyond our control. Why not rely on it now? Why not take a chance on going by what you feel inside?

In our lives one time or another, we have felt the enormous live saving moment of our gut instinct.

A last second escape from a killing accident, a last minute decision to not pursue that job offer which helped you save your career from a company that shut down in a months' time – we cannot really put our fingers to what gut instinct is about but what we can be sure about that is IT EXISTS and WORKS!

Your gut instinct works for your benefit. It ensures your safety – in all spheres of your life. Sometimes your instincts will whisper, other times your instinct screams. If you pay close attention, you can hear their guidance and change your life's routes accordingly.

Instinct-based decision making is faster, less stressful, and more holistic. So if you've been making all of your decisions based on rational analysis but you're not

100% happy with the results, try following going with your gut feel for a change.

Chapter 27: Oprah On Self-esteem

Self-esteem comes from being able to define the world in your own terms and refusing to abide by the judgments of others.

People are often confused about what it means to have self-esteem. Some think it has to do with the way you look or how popular you are with your friends or others. Others believe that having a great body will help you gain self-esteem, while others think you actually need to have accomplished something in order to have good self-esteem.

Boiled down to its simplicity, self-esteem simply means appreciating yourself for who you are — faults, foibles and all. It seems like other cultures don't grapple with self-esteem as much as Americans do, perhaps because of the emphasis we seem to put on materialistic indicators of self-worth (like what kind of car you drive, what school your kids attend, what your grades are, how big a house you have, or what your title is at work).

If you want to live your best life, you should care the least about what people have to say on your back. From the way you look to walk to act – there are always some people ready to criticize you. It is your life and it is your body. No matter how you look or how you walk – if you own it up like a queen – if you radiate grace through your imperfections, you can win this world.

Chapter 28: Oprah On Hard Work

The big secret in life is there is no secret. Whatever your goal, you can get there if you're willing to work.

Every day that goes by you either move closer towards achieving a goal or you move further away from that goal. If you take specific steps you can be assured that you are moving towards your goal. If you do nothing you are moving away from the goal. By being still, you lose momentum, and the level of inertia of our current position increases.

If you just believe in the power of attraction, it is going to take a lot of time for you to achieve what you want. Just by keep repeating weeds are gone, weeds are gone is not going to help eradicate weeds from your garden. You got to get up and put in the necessary work.

If you are not willing to work for what you want – you are never going to get it. It is as simple as that. Your goal might be to marry that man or a woman, you have to work on that goal, you have to invest in that relationship, you have show your commitment and love and loyalty and earnestness which will help you reach your goal.

If you want that high paying job, just chanting I am getting that job, I am getting that job is not going to help either. You have to invest in yourself, you have to learn the necessary skillsets that job requires of you. Only if you are ready to get out and put in the necessary work that is needed for you to succeed – you can become a success.

Chapter 29: Success Quotes & Lessons from Oprah

Think like a queen. A queen is not afraid to fail. Failure is another stepping stone to greatness.

We can't become what we need to be by remaining what we are.

⍰

Dogs are my favorite role models. I want to work like a dog, doing what I was born to do with joy and purpose. I want to play like a dog, with total, jolly abandon. I want to love like a dog, with unabashed devotion and complete lack of concern about what people do for a living, how much money they have or how much they weigh. The fact that we still live with dogs, even when we don't have to herd or hunt our dinner, gives me hope for humans and canines alike.

❓

The great courageous act that we must all do, is to have the courage to step out of our history and past so that we can live our dreams

❓

Self esteem comes from being able to define the world in your own terms and refusing to abide by the judgments of others.

❓

When I look at the future, it's so bright it burns my eyes

❓

You are responsible for your life. You can't keep blaming somebody else for your dysfunction. Life is really about moving on

Forgiveness is giving up the hope that the past could have been any different.

Doing the best at this moment puts you in the best place for the next moment

⟨?⟩

Only make decisions that support your self-image, self-esteem and self-worth

Every day brings a chance to live free of regret and with as much joy, fun and laughter as you can stand.

⟨?⟩

As you become more clear about who you really are, you'll be better able to decide what is best for you – the first time around

❓

Do the one thing you think you cannot do. Fail at it. Try again. Do better the second time. The only people who never tumble are those who never mount the high wire.

The whole point of being alive is to evolve into the complete person you were intended to be

❓

I know for sure that what we dwell on is who we become

❓

It makes no difference how many peaks you reach if there was no pleasure in the climb.

❓

Meditate. Breathe consciously. Listen. Pay attention. Treasure every moment. Make the connection.

You look at yourself and you accept yourself for who you are, and once you accept yourself for who you are you become a better person.

You have to find what sparks a light in you so that you in your own way can illuminate the world.

The big secret in life is there is no secret. Whatever your goal, you can et there is you're willing to work.

If you want your life to be more rewarding, you have to change the way you think

To love yourself is a never-ending journey

I believe the choice to be excellent begins with aligning your thoughts and words with the intention to require more from yourself

﹖

Follow your instincts. That's where true wisdom manifests itself

﹖

In the midst of Difficulty lies Opportunity

﹖

I am grateful for the blessings of wealth but it has not changed who I am. My feet are still on the ground. I'm just wearing better shoes.

Education is the key to unlocking the world, a passport to freedom.

❓

With every experience, you alone are painting your own canvas, thought by thought, choice by choice.

❓

Mr.Right is coming, but he's in Africa and he's walking

❓

So go ahead. Fall down. The world looks different from the ground

❓

Everything happens for a reason, even when we are not wise enough to see it. When there is no struggle, there is no strength.

The best of times is NOW

❓

It doesn't matter who you are, where you come from. The ability to triumph begins with you – always.

❓

I've learned not to worry about what might come next

❓

I am a woman in process. I am just trying like everybody else. I try to take every conflict, every experience, and learn from it. Life is never dull.

❓

I don't believe in failure. It's not failure if you enjoy the process.

❓

I finally realized that being grateful to my body was key to giving more love to myself

You are built not to shrink down to less but to blossom into more

❓

What god intended for you goes far beyond anything you can imagine

❓

Every one of us gets through the tough times because somebody is there, standing in the gap to close it for us.

❓

Life is about becoming more of who you really are...

You face the biggest challenge of all; to have the courage to seek your big dream regardless of what anyone says. You are the only person alive who can see your big picture and even you can't see it all.

※

Difficulties come when you don't pay attention to life's whisper. Life always whispers to you first, but if you ignore the whisper, sooner or later you'll get a scream.

※

The happiness you feel is in direct proportion to the love you give.

※

I will tell you that there have been no failures in my life. I don't want to sound like some metaphysical queen, but there have been no failures. There have been some tremendous lessons.

※

Live your best life.

Always take a stand for yourself, your values. You're defined by what you stand for.

❓

When you know better, you do better…

I was once afraid of people saying 'who does she think she is?' now I have the courage to stand and say, 'this is who I am'

❓

Books were my pass to personal freedom. I learned to read at age three and there discovered was a whole world to conquer that went beyond our farm in Mississippi.

The essential question is not, 'how busy are you'? but 'what are you busy at'?. Are you doing what fulfills you?

❓

Devote today to something so daring even you can't believe you're doing it

What other people label or might try to call failure, I have learned is just God's way of pointing you in a new direction

Follow your feelings. If it feels right, move forward. If it doesn't feel right, don't do it.

The roles we play in each other's lives are only as powerful as the trust and connection between us – the protection, safety and caring we are willing to share.

Create the highest, grandest vision possible for your life, because you become what you believe.

If you neglect to recharge a battery, it dies. And if you run full speed ahead without stopping for water, you lose momentum to finish the race.

"I had no idea that being your authentic self could make me as rich as I've become. If I had, I'd have done it a lot earlier."

※

"Excellence is the best deterrent to racism or sexism."

※

"Your gut is your inner compass. Whenever you have to consult with other people for an answer, you're headed in the wrong direction."

※

"The surest way to bring goodness to yourself is to make it your intention to do good for somebody else."

"The more you praise and celebrate your life, the more there is in life to celebrate."

"Sometimes in the thick of life, when my call list is longer than the day and people are lined up waiting for meeting after meeting, I just stop. I still myself. And look at a tree. A flower. The sun's light reflecting off the window. And I remember love is available. I inhale it, exhale, and get back to work."

⁂

"Surround yourself with only people who are going to lift you higher."

⁂

"You know you are on the road to success if you would do your job, and not be paid for it."

⁂

"This is your moment. Own it."

⁂

"We're each responsible for our own life. No one else is or even could be."

Connect, embrace, literate. Love somebody. Just one person. And then spread to two. And as many as you can. You'll see the difference it makes.

What I love most about reading; it gives you the ability to reach higher ground. And keep climbing.

Know this for sure: when you get the chance, go for it.

Improving your life doesn't have to be about changing everything – its about making changes that count.

You can either waltz boldly onto the stage of life and live the way you know your spirit is nudging you to, or you can sit quietly by the wall, receding into the shadows of fear and self-doubt

People believe marriage will make us better!

I always knew I was destined for greatness.

There's a difference between thinking you deserve to be happy and knowing that you are worthy of being happy. Your being alive makes worthiness your birthright. You alone are enough.

"Living in the moment brings you a sense of reverence for all of life's blessings.

There is no fun than helping to make someone's dreams come true. Especially when that person is ayoung person and who really want it and really dserve it

Here's the gift of gratitude: In order to feel it, your ego has to take a backseat. What shows up in its place is greater compassion and understanding. Instead of being frustrated, you choose appreciation. And the more grateful you become , the more you have to be grateful for

We go through life discovering the truth about who we are and determining who has earned the right to share the space within our heart. And now I simply want to share what I've been given. I want to continue to encourage as many people as I can to open their hearts to life, because if I know anything for sure, it's that opening my heart is what has brought me the greatest success and joy

What I learned for sure was that holding the shame was the greatest burden of all. When you have nothing to be ashamed of, when you know who you are and what you stand for, you stand in wisdom.

Whenever I'm faced with a difficult decision, I ask myself: What would I do if I weren't afraid of making a mistake, feeling rejected, looking foolish, or being alone? I know for sure that when you remove the fear, the answer you've been searching for comes into focus.

Here's how I see your weight—it is your smoke detector. And we're all burning up the best part of our lives." I'd never thought of it that way before, but it was a true aha moment. My weight was an indicator warning, a flashing light blaring my disconnection from the center of myself.

I want people to understand, that you are responsible for your life. Weather you are transexual, weather you are a divorcee, weather you are terminally ill, weather you are posessed by the devil or trying to get the devil out of you. You have control over your life, and it is only when you recognize that, and is willing to be responsible for your life that you can truely soar, and I believe that it's possible in our lifetime to fly if you want to.

Energy is the essence of life. Every day you decide how you're going to use it by knowing what you want and what it takes to reach that goal, and by maintaining focus.

By the time I was 17, I was working in radio, making $100 a week. And that's when I made my peace with money. I decided that no matter what job I ever did, I wanted that same feeling I got when I first started in radio—the feeling of I love this so much, even if you didn't pay me I'd show up every day, on time and happy to be here. I recognized then what I know now for sure: If you can get paid for doing what you love, every paycheck is a bonus. Give yourself the bonus of a lifetime: Pursue your passion. Discover what you love. Then do it!

When we hold secrets it creates shame, and shame is a great barrier to success because when you carry the shame you do not allow yourself to fulfill your greatest potential, you do not honour the truth of yourself, you do not honour what is your highest self. When you let go of the secret allows you to live to your full potential.

Become the change you want to see—those are words I live by. Instead of belittling, uplift.

Only moment you have for certain. I hope you aren't so wrapped up in nonessential stuff that you forget to really enjoy yourself—because this moment is about to be over.

When you know for sure that you're on course and doing exactly what you're supposed to be doing, fulfilling your soul's intention, your heart's desire. When your life is on course with its purpose, you are at your most powerful. And though you may stumble, you will not fall.

There is no greater gift you can give or receive than to honor your calling. Its why you were born. And how you become most truly alive.

No matter what challenge you may be facing, you must remember that while the canvas of your life is painted with daily experiences, behaviors, reactions, and emotions, you're the one controlling the brush. If I had known this at 21, I could have saved myself a lot of heartache and self-doubt. It would have been a revelation to understand that we are all the artists of our own lives—and that we can use as many colors and brushstrokes as we like.

For sure we live in a youth-obsessed culture that is constantly trying to tell us that if we're not young and glowing and "hot," we don't matter. But I refuse to buy into such a distorted view of reality. And I would never lie about or deny my age. To do so is to contribute to a sickness pervading our society—the sickness of wanting to be what you're not. I know for sure that only by owning who and what you are can you step into the fullness of life. I feel sorry for anyone who buys into the myth that you can be what you once were. The way to your best life isn't denial. It's owning every moment and staking a claim to the here and now. You're not the same woman you were a decade ago; if you're lucky, you're not the same woman you were last year. The whole point of aging, as I see it, is change. If we let them, our experiences can keep teaching us about ourselves. I celebrate that. Honor it. Hold it in reverence. And I'm grateful for every age I'm blessed to become.

What I know for sure: There is no need to struggle with your body when you can make a loving and grateful peace with it.

Whenever I'm faced with a difficult decision, I ask myself: What would I do if I weren't afraid of making a mistake, feeling rejected, looking foolish, or being alone? I know for sure that when you remove the fear, the answer you've been searching for comes into focus. And as you walk into what you fear, you should know for sure that your deepest struggle can, if you're willing and open, produce your greatest strength.

In every job I've taken and every city in which I've lived, I have known that it's time to move on when I've grown as much as I can. Sometimes moving on terrified me. But always it taught me that the true meaning of courage is to be afraid, and then, with your knees knocking, to step out anyway. Making a bold move is the only way to advance toward the grandest vision the universe has for you. If you allow it, fear will completely immobilize you. And once it has you in its grip, it will fight to keep you from ever becoming your best self.

Books, for me, used to be a way to escape. I now consider reading a good book a sacred indulgence, a chance to be any place I choose. It is my absolute favorite way to spend time. What I know for sure is that reading opens you up. It exposes you and gives you access to anything your mind can hold. What I love most about reading: It gives you the ability to reach higher ground. And keep climbing.

I urge you to pursue preserving your personal history to allow your children and grandchildren to know who you were as a child and what your hopes and dreams were

What I know for sure is that every day brings a chance for you to draw in a breath, kick off your shoes, and step out and dance—to live free of regret and filled with as much joy, fun, and laughter as you can stand. You can either waltz boldly onto the stage of life and live the way you know your spirit is nudging you to, or you can sit quietly by the wall, receding into the shadows of fear and self-doubt. You

One of the most important questions a woman can ask herself: What do I really want-and what is my spirit telling me is the best way to proceed?

Don't back down just to keep the peace. Standing up for yourself builds self confidence and self esteem.

At different times in our journeys, if we're paying attention, we get to sing the song we're meant to sing in the perfect key of life.

I will just create, and if it works, it works, and if it doesn't, I'll create something else. I don't have any limitations on what I think I could do or be.

Every day brings a chance for you to draw in a breath, kick off your shoes and dance

You get in life what you have the courage to ask for

Cheers to a new year and another chance for us to get it right

Surround yourself only with people who are going to take you higher

The more you praise and celebrate your life, the more there is in life to celebrate

Breathe. Let go. And remind yourself that this very moment is the only one you know you have for sure

I trust that everything happens for a reason, even if we are not wise enough to see it

Real integrity is doing the right thing, knowing that nobody's going to know whether you did it or not

I've come to believe that each of us has a personal calling that's as unique as a fingerprint – and that the best way to succeed is to discover what you love and then find a way to offer it to others in the form of service, working hard and also allowing the energy of the universe to lead you.

If a man wants you, nothing can keep him away. If he doesn't want you, nothing can make him stay

Chapter 30: How To Use This Book Effectively?

I hope you have enjoyed this Book. I sincerely believe the Success Lessons detailed here will help you move ahead in your life.

Whatever your dreams may be – be it professional or personal – if you strongly believe in it and work on it, you can make it happen.

Reading a self-help book alone will not help you in your success or development in life. You have to start practicing what you read.

So take these 125 success lessons to your heart. Try to read atleast 1 lesson each day and start following the principles mentioned in that lesson.

I assure you, if you follow this, the kind of change you will be seeing in your life would be astounding.

Wishing you more & most in life! Be the Awesome YOU forever!

Upcoming Books On "Life & Success Lessons" from

- Anthony Robins
- Jim Rohn
- Les Brown
- Brian Tracy
- Dale Carnegie
- Jake Canfield
- Deepak Chopra
- Elon Musk
- Richard Branson
- Donald Trump
- Steve Jobs
- Mark Zuckerberg
- Winston Churchill
- Abraham Lincoln

******

For More Books on Personal Development, Self Help & Inspiring Biographies, Search "TONY ROHN" in Amazon

******

--THE END--